The Hairdresser's Baby

By Amy Watson
Illustrated by Drew McClure

Turner Publishing
Paducah, Kentucky

Acknowledgements

Lee McClure

Phillip Bryan

Tina Darnell Baker

Betty Riley

Tonya Holshouser

Mark Workman

WPSD-TV

PUBLISHING COMPANY

412 Broadway • P.O. Box 3101
Paducah, Kentucky 42002-3101
(270) 443-0121
www.turnerpublishing.com

Second Edition

Copyright © 2003 Amy Watson
Publishing Rights: Turner Publishing Company

This book or any part thereof may not be reproduced
without the written consent of the author and the publisher.

Turner Publishing Company Staff:
Shelley R. Davidson, Designer

Library of Congress Control Number:
2003107944
ISBN: 1-56311-906-4

Printed in the United States of America.
Limited Edition.

To my husband and children, for making me a wife and mother— my greatest accomplishments.

To my parents, for teaching me that family is a great accomplishment.

One day, Shampooville was all-a-suds
over the latest gossip.

Someone said...
    that she heard...
        that someone saw...
            that the beauty shop was closing!

Shampooville was a tiny town
but it was big on STYLE
thanks to the beauty shop's hairdresser.

The townspeople needed her
to keep them on top of the trends.

In fact, the beauty shop was like
Shampooville's City Hall
and the hairdresser was the
Mayor of Mane.

Everyone copied
the hairdresser's fashion ideas...

even the people's pets!

"I bet she closed the shop
because of her baby," whispered Wilma.

"I heard her baby doesn't have any hair," added Becky.

"I heard that, too," continued Connie
over conversation at the coffeehouse.

"How tragic!" offered Olivia. "A hairdresser
with a baby with no hair? What an odd pair!"

11

The hairdresser's baby was very cute.

She had pretty, blue eyes.

She had a little, tiny nose.

But, she DIDN'T have any hair!

"A lot of babies are bald," thought the hairdresser.

"It will grow."

The BABY grew.

Her feet, her hands, her legs and her arms grew.

But, her HAIR didn't grow!

The baby learned to
walk
talk
play
laugh
and
to *love*.

But, her hair hadn't grown any!

The hairdresser asked her doctor for advice.

After a checkup,
the doctor had some troubling news.

The doctor said, "Your baby has a condition."

"She has
nohairsagrowin-sillyosis."

19

The hairdresser was now bothered
and
WORRIED.

"My baby with no hair!!!!

What will people think about a hairdresser
with a baby with no hair?"

The hairdresser was very upset.

She took the baby home
and closed her shop for a week.

She wouldn't even crack a curtain.

And on the streets of Shampooville,
there was a dramatic change.

Without a beauty expert,

The people looked...

very different!

One morning, as the hairdresser was missing
the cutting and combing and curling,
she opened her curtains.

She couldn't believe her eyes!

The streets of Shampooville were a
shaggy mess!

"It's time to get back to work
and clean up this town!" she said.

Right at that moment,
the hairdresser's baby
held out her arms.

The hairdresser picked her up,
hugged and kissed her
and looked into her pretty, blue eyes.

And FINALLY
the hairdresser realized
she'd been bothered
and WORRIED
about something that really didn't matter much.

And, she began to cry.

After a few minutes

the hairdresser wiped her tears

and opened her eyes to...

HER GREATEST FASHION IDEA EVER!

The next day
the hairdresser reopened her shop
extra early.

After a few initial "Ooooohs" and "Oh mys!"
from her customers,

the hairdresser spent her busiest day yet

CUTTING
and
SMOOTHING
and
SHINING!

That evening
all of Shampooville
had a NEW look...

...even the hairdresser.

The Author

Amy Watson grew up in Murray, Kentucky. She graduated from Murray State University with a degree in journalism in 1989. Amy has worked as a News Anchor/Reporter at WPSD-TV in Paducah, Kentucky since 1993, where she's earned a number of awards for newswriting, including Best Reporter by the Associated Press. Amy lives in Paducah with her husband and three children.

Amy's inspiration for the book came from a true story. A former hairdresser from Murray had a baby with a medical condition preventing the baby from growing hair for several years. Amy remembers the hairdresser saying, "Can you believe this? A hairdresser with a baby with no hair. What an odd pair!"

Amy's love for reading to her children motivated her to write this book, and she says, "My talented nephew actually brought the story to life with his amazing pictures."

The Illustrator

Drew McClure discovered his love for the visual arts at an early age. Inspired by Mark Kistler (Imagination Station) during kindergarten enrichment classes in southern California, he found the fine arts from seeds planted in cartooning. He has since developed a broad range of skills in multiple media. A graduate of the Kentucky Governor's School for the Arts, he studied under nationally recognized artists in refining his craft. He has received first place honors in state high school art competition and is a featured young artist in the Paducah, Kentucky Area. He is currently a Senior at Heath High School and Senior Captain of the Paducah Swim Team.

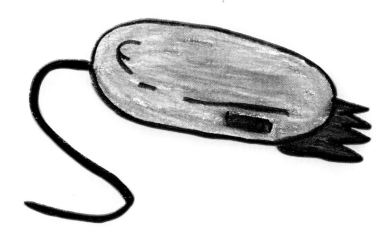

The End!